SQUADRONS!

No. 3

THE SUPERMARINE
SPITFIRE MK. V

IN THE FAR EAST

PHIL H. LISTEMANN

Layout & project design: Phil Listemann

ISBN: 978-2918590-37-8

Copyright

© 2014 Philedition - Phil Listemann

revised - 2015

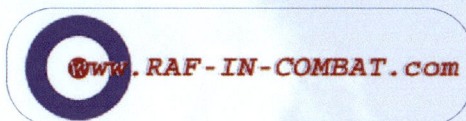

Colour profiles: Gaetan Marie/Bravo Bravo Aviation

Contributors & Acknowledgments:
Hugh Halliday, Drew Harrison, Paul Sortehaug, Andrew Thomas.

GLOSSARY OF TERMS

PERSONEL :

(AUS)/RAF: Australian serving in the RAF
(BEL)/RAF: Belgian serving in the RAF
(CAN)/RAF: Canadian serving in the RAF
(CZ)/RAF: Czechoslovak serving in the RAF
(NFL)/RAF: Newfoundlander serving in the RAF
(NL)/RAF: Dutch serving in the RAF
(NZ)/RAF: New Zealander serving in the RAF
(POL)/RAF: Pole serving in the RAF
(RHO)/RAF: Rhodesian serving in the RAF
(SA)/RAF: South African serving in the RAF
(US)/RAF - RCAF : American serving in the RAF or RCAF

RANKS

G/C : Group Captain
W/C : Wing Commander
S/L : Squadron Leader
F/L : Flight Lieutenant
F/O : Flying Officer
P/O : Pilot Officer
W/O : Warrant Officer
F/Sgt : Flight Sergeant
Sgt : Sergeant
Cpl : Corporal
LAC : Leading Aircraftman

OTHER

CO : Commander
DFC : Distinguished Flying Cross
DFM : Distinguished Flying Medal
DSO : Distinguished Service Order
Eva. : Evaded
ORB : Operational Record Book
OTU : Operational Training Unit
PoW : Prisoner of War
PAF: Polish Air Force
RAF : Royal Air Force
RAAF : Royal Australian Air Force
RCAF : Royal Canadian Air Force
RNZAF : Royal New Zealand Air Force
SAAF : South African Air Force
Sqn : Squadron
† : Killed

CODENAMES - OFFENSIVE OPERATIONS - FIGHTER COMMAND

CIRCUS:
Bombers heavily escorted by fighters, the purpose being to bring enemy fighters into combat.

RAMROD:
Bombers escorted by fighters, the primary aim being to destroy a target.

RANGER:
Large formation freelance intrusion over enemy territory with aim of wearing down enemy figthers.

RHUBARD:
Freelance fighter sortie against targets of opportunity.

RODEO:
A fighter sweep without bombers.

SWEEP:
An offensive flight by fighters designed to draw up and clear the enemy from the sky.

THE SPITFIRE V
IN THE FAR EAST

The Spitfire Mk.V was one the major marks of this famous fighter and formed the backbone of RAF Fighter Command in 1941 and 1942. When the Focke-Wulf Fw190 was introduced, in Western Europe at the end of 1941, the Mk.V was outclassed and a successor – the Mk.IX – had to be found very quickly. This was not the end of the career of the Mk.V in the RAF, however, and the mark, still a potent fighter, was seen as capable of giving good service in many other theatres. Construction of the Mk.V continued in large numbers well into 1943 because of the slow introduction of the Mk.IX. The Mk.V was therefore sent overseas, first to North Africa and Malta where it became a major asset for the RAF and became the only day fighter employed by Autumn 1942. It was later introduced in limited numbers over Darwin, Australia, and proved successful against the Japanese.

By mid-1943, therefore, the Spitfire Mk.V was present everywhere the RAF was fighting except for the Far East theatre. Up to that time the RAF's modest fighter force in the region had managed to hold the line mainly with Hurricanes andtwo squadrons of Mohawks. The Mohawk was totally obsolete and on its way out and the Hurricane, as a pure fighter, was not far behind the American fighter. The growing obsolescence of the RAF's fighters was accelerated when the Japanese began to introduce new fighter types over Burma. The need to reinforce the air defence of key areas of India was soon seen as essential by many even though the threat of an invasion of India had faded. The arrival of the Spitfire was part of the buildup of reinforcements for the RAF in the Far East. This was part of the Allies' aim to re-take Burma and, later on, Malaya. This necessity, and the availability of some Spitfire Mk.VCs, led the diversion of about 80 aircraft to equip three fighter squadrons. This was a stop-gap measure, however, pending the arrival en masse of the Spitfire Mk.VIII which had been issued to the Mediterranean theatre as a priority. The Mk.VCs – 76 of them – arrived in India between August and November 1943 as follows:

August 1943: JG865, JL108, JL303, JL317, JL319 - JL322, JL331, JL334, LZ939, LZ971 - LZ973, LZ975, MA263, MA265, MA286, MA288, MA290, MA292, MA296, MA297, MA341, MA347 - MA349, MA361, MA365, MA367, MA368, MA383, MA384, MA386, MA388, MA390 - MA393, MA396, MA650, MA652, MA654, MA670, MA672, MA674 - MA677, MA686, MA688, MA692, MA694, MA651, MA652, MA857, MA899, MA902, MA903, MH299 - MH300, MH305, MH308 **(63)**.
September 1943: MA364, MH637 - MH640 **(5)**.
November 1943 : JG714, MA284, MA696, MH301 - MH303, MH311, MH641 **(8)**.

The Spitfire Mk.V was used in India by Nos.136, 607 and 615 Squadrons but only for a relatively short period of time. By summer 1944 the survivors had been withdrawn from use but not before having responded well to the requirements of the RAF in the region. In all around 3,000 sorties were flown and over 70 claims made. After July 1944 the extent of Mk.V use is not known with certainty because of the destruction of many records at war's end. Some were used by the Air Fighting Training Unit (AFTU) or 3 RFU (Refresher Flying Unit) but, overall, the Mk.Vs seem to have been quickly replaced by Mk.VIIIs. Given that large numbers of Mk.VIIIs were delivered to the theatre, and that shortages of spare parts for some types was a recurring problem in the Far East, it is logical to suppose that most surviving Mk.Vs were stored to be used as spares sources. Indeed half of the original complement, around 40, survived. This was enough to support one squadron for a reasonable period but the RAF chose not to do so. The only logical explanation is the lack of spare parts availability, and it is probable that no parts were scheduled to be shipped out because of priority being given to other types, obliging the RAF in the Far East to restrict use of the Mk.Vs to a minimum and then holding many of them in reserve in case of an emergency (something which never occurred). Many were simply struck off charge (SOC) either when a major overhaul had to be undertaken and when VJ-Day took place.

In early 1945 some Mk.Vs were condemned by batch - eight in February (MA297, MA348, MA388, MA392, MA652, MA676, MA686, MH311) and eight others in April (MA286, MA341, MA368, MA391, MA654, MA674, MA675, MH300). Taking accident and administrative losses into account only the following Mk.V aircraft were still in RAF hands in the region at the end of August 1945: JL303, JL334, MA290, MA341, MA361, MA368, MA396, MA692, MH642. Even these aircraft did not survive that long after that, but some did until spring 1946. MA361 seem to have a late SOC date (1947) but this was probably an administrative error as the type had been declared obsolete in England for some time. The Far East was a tiny piece of the Mk.V war tally but its introduction in the region was a success. There is no doubt the Spitfire helped the Allies to establish definitively air supremacy in Burma.

Spitfire Mk.VC MA383, devoid of codes, one of the first allocated to 136 Sqn and first flown by the CO, S/L Constantine. Note the large SEAC roundels, rarely painted on Spitfires and soon abandoned.
(via Andrew Thomas)

Victories - confirmed or probable claims: 35.0

First operational sortie: 03.12.43	**Number of sorties:** ca. 560
Last operational sortie: 29.02.44	**Total aircraft written-off: 8**

Aircraft lost on operations: 7
Aircraft lost in accidents: 1

Squadron code letters:
HM

COMMANDING OFFICERS

S/L Alexander N. CONSTANTINE	RAF No.40893	(AUS)/RAF	...	...

SQUADRON USAGE

136 Squadron was a Hurricane squadron, led by S/L Noel Constantine, when it was selected to convert to the Spitfire. This unit had been fighting in the Far East since it was sent as a reinforcement at the end of 1941. The squadron took charge of its first Spitfire Mk.Vs on 10 October while based at Baigachi in India. The CO made the unit's first flight, a 20 minute test at midday, on the type. It is worth noting that the squadron was still flying the Hurricane on operations while converting to the Spitfire. Training began in earnest on the 15th with pilots, one by one, starting to practice on the Spitfire. By the end of the month every pilot had made at least a couple of flights on the type. On 6 November the pilots and machines were sent to Armada Road to complete their training (air and ground firing). The timing of this was poor as, over the following days, many machines had to be sent back singly to Baigachi to undertake a 40 hour inspection (something which could have been anticipated before moving the squadron to Armada Road!). On 15 November the Squadron lost its first Spitfire while conducting practice attacks. Flight Sergeant Clarke experienced trouble with the engine of MA288 and was obliged to make a forced-landing 15 miles from the aerodrome. The Spitfire was only fit for scrapping while Clarke escaped major injuries. The rest of the month was uneventful and over 350 hours on Spitfires were logged in November. The Squadron was now ready for operations.

By then the Squadron had moved forward to Burma and was eventually stationed at Ramu/Lyons for operations. It wasn't long before the first scramble was carried out on 3 December. Pilots F/O Greville Moorhouse

Noel Constantine was an Australian from Victoria who joined the RAF in 1938, initially serving as a Defiant pilot with 141 Sqn in 1940. He volunteered for an overseas posting and in 1943 became OC of 273 Sqn before taking command of 136 Sqn in June that same year. He was to make all his claims with the unit relinquishing command of it in March 1944 by which time it was flying Mk.VIII Spitfires. He was killed in 1947 when the civil registered Dakota he was flying into New Guinea was shot down by two Dutch P-40s.
(Andrew Thomas)

4

Eric Brown (left), like Constantine, made all his claims with 136 Sqn, with which he had served since September 1941. He was shot down twice before being shot down a third time and killed on 15 February 1944. The award of his DFC had been gazetted only a week previously. (Andrew Thomas)

Arthur Conway (below), a Londoner, had the same route as Brown and joined the 136 Sqn in October 1941. He survived the war being credited with 7 confirmed kills, all but two while flying Spitfire Mk.Vs, His two earlier kills were obtained piloting Hurricanes. By November 1943 he was a Flight Commander with a DFC. He left the squadron in March 1944 at the end of his tour and returned to operations leading 155 Sqn during the closing stages of the war in the Far East. He served in the post-war RAF retiring in 1976. (Andrew Thomas)

and F/Sgt William Cousens (RAAF) reported an uneventful flight. Later that day 10 aircraft scrambled to intercept an enemy aircraft spotted 100 miles from the base but this flight, too, was uneventful – the 'bogey' was actually found to be a friendly aircraft – except for F/L Peter Speller who had to pancake his aircraft while taking off causing slight damage which was repaired afterwards. Two days later 10 pilots rushed to their machines for a scramble. After patrolling west of Cox's Bazaar the Squadron returned to base but F/L Eric Brown was able to intercept the enemy aircraft, a formation consisting of about 40 bombers with fighter escort, 80 miles west of the Maishkal Islands. He attacked one of the Ki-21s, which he claimed as destroyed, but, having flown at the very limit of his aircraft's endurance, was obliged to make a forced landing while running out of fuel. The aircraft was subsequently declared damaged beyond economical repair. If the destruction of this first Japanese aircraft was highly welcomed the loss of a precious Spitfire in such circumstances wasn't seen so positively.

Nothing important was reported until the 26th when the whole wing scrambled – 136 Squadron provided 12 Spitfires – to inter-

On the left, the New Zealander of Maori parentage from Tonga, Johnny Rudling who made one of 136 Sqn's first claims when he shot down a Sally bomber on 26 December 1943. He has been awarded the DFM in November. However he was later lost, flying a Spitfire Mk.VIII during an engagement with enemy fighters, on 29 April 1944, after going to the aid of a fellow pilot. (Andrew thomas)

On the right, another Kiwi, 'Viv' Jacobs, who served with the 136 between 1941 and 1944. On Hurricanes he claimed one Japanese bomber as probably destroyed and four aircraft damaged in 1943, but on Spitfire V, he would make one claim only, a damaged Zero on 15 January 1944. (J.D. Rudling via P.Sortehaug)

cept a formation of 21 Ki-21s, escorted by 78 Ki-43s, sent to attack Chittagong. Two pilots of the Squadron were able to intercept the force - F/Sgt 'Bob' Cross claiming two Ki-21s west of the town and P/O 'Johnny' Rudling claiming another. However, for the latter, the interception ended in a bad way as he was shot-up by Ki-43s and he had to make a forced landing during which his aircraft ground-looped. The year was not over for 136 Squadron as another attack on the Arakan area was soon reported. The Spitfires of the Wing had taken off at around 10.55 and climbed to 30,000 feet before being vectored onto the raiders near St Martin's island. Here the Japanese aircraft were spotted 9,000 feet below and in the ensuing fight nine Spitfire pilots claimed eight Ki-21s and three Ki-43s shot down, three more bombers and one fighter as probably shot down and four fighters damaged. All for no loss ! Flight Lieutenant Conway was most successful among the victors with two 'Sally' bombers destroyed, one 'Oscar' fighter destroyed, one more probably destroyed and one Oscar damaged. In return the Squadron lost one Spitfire, that flown by F/L Eric Brown (again!) – Brown's aircraft was damaged in the engine by return fire from a bomber. Again, though, he succeeded in making a belly landing on a beach at Japipara. The aircraft was a write-off. December was a month to remember in 136 Squadron's annals with 17 aircraft shot down, four more probably shot down and nine damaged against two Spitfires lost in combat and no human loss.

Despite these successes the association with the Spitfire Mk.V had already begun to come to an end in January. Indeed, during the first days of 1944, the CO performed a battle climb to40,000 feet in a Spitfire Mk.VIII. Operational flights had to be continued on the Mk.Vs pending the delivery of further, far more capable, Mk.VIII aircraft. In the meantime, for their recent actions against the Japanese, F/L Eric Brown and F/Sgt Robert Cross were recommended for immediate awards of a DFC and DFM respectively. While the squadron's pilots gained experience on the Mk.VIII for the rest of the month the unit was called for scrambles many times up to 15 January. On that day the Japanese returned in force over the area but, this time, launched fighter sweeps instead of bombing raids which had proved to be costly. The Squadron scrambled once more with twelve aircraft at 08.00 and climbed to 24,000 feet from where they were vectored to Maungdaw. The pilots reported two formations, each of 12 or more fighters, at 15,000 feet. It was F/L Gordon Conway who led the attack for 136 Squadron as he had two weeks previously. The Japanese suffered severe losses to the Spitfires - 136 Squadron alone claiming five fighters destroyed two more 'probables', and two damaged. The most successful pilot, F/L Garvan, claimed two destroyed, one probable and one damaged. However, in contrast to the success of 31 December, the Japanese were effective this time against the Spitfires as Garvan's aircraft (MH637) was hit and he was forced to make a soft crash-landing in a paddy field. Less fortunate was F/O Derek Fuge who was killed in his aircraft. The next day 136 Squadron was called up again to intercept an enemy formation reported over the Maugdaw area. Squadron Leader Constantine sighted a dozen aircraft flying over a wide area, 10,000 feet below and ahead of the Squadron, heading west over the first ridge of hills south-east of Maugdaw. The CO went into the attack with the rest of the section and in the ensuing mêlée five more fighters were claimed as destroyed and three damaged with the CO taking his share

> Spitfire V coded 'R' of No. 136 Squadron at the end of 1943. The serial cannot be read in full, a M or H only, but at that time, R was MH308. R was later used by JG714 when MH308 was passed on to 607 Squadron in January 1944. The squadron codes letters HM were introduced early in 1944. *(ww2images.com)*

Another group of successful pilots photographed on 15 January 1944: The CO, S/L Constantine seated on the wing, then left to right, F/O Dudley Barnett of New South Wales, Australia, F/Sgt Frank Wilding, F/L Arthur Conway and F/O Denis Garvan. The Spitfire Mk.V coded E is probably MA365 which was lost just a couple of days later. *(Drew Harrison)*

with one destroyed and one damaged. The next three days were passed on practice and testing new aircraft but on the 20th the Squadron was involved in its last major engagement flying the Mk.V. Eleven Spitfires were scrambled but two had to return early (F/O Greville Moorhouse and F/Sgt Reginald Clarke - RNZAF) – 136 Sqn attacked from up-sun and in about 15 minutes shot down five Japanese aircraft. Four more were claimed as probable and six damaged with the most successful pilot once

Two Canadians who scored on 31 December 1943, left 'Dopey' LeCraw and right 'Vern' Butler. Both arrived in the Far East in 1942 with No. 136 Squadron and were engared against the Japanese over Burma during the intinial combats.
After a long tour, LeCraw would lead B Flight and left in May 1944 to become a flight instructor at No. 1 SFTS, but Vern Butler was killed before the end of his tour, being shot down and killed by an Oscar on 17.03.44. He was one of the first pilots to be killed on a Spitfire Mk. VIII in the Far East.
(LeCraw - J.D. Rudling via P.Sortehaug)

again being the CO with one destroyed, three probable and one damaged. F/O Garvan followed with one destroyed, one probable and one damaged but was slightly wounded in the arm and leg in the process. The Japanese fighters shot down F/Sgt Peter Kennedy's Spitfire. He was sadly killed while descending in his parachute.

By the end of the month the Squadron slowly began to introduce the Mk.VIII on operations. However the main operational activity remained on the Mk.V because some pilots still had to gain experience on the Mk.VIII and this situation lasted into February. On 5 February F/Sgt Arthur Kearon, an Irishman like Kennedy, was posted missing following an interception. As they had dived to attack the Spitfires were caught by Japanese fighters and, from this initial action, the pilots lost sight of Kearon. Only a damaged 'Hamp' was claimed by W/O Frank Wilding in return. Another combat took place four days later during which one aircraft was destroyed by F/Sgt Cross (flying a Mk.VIII) and four more claimed as damaged by Cross and two other pilots. The CO was frustrated as he had to come back early, due to engine trouble, and missed the chance to add to his tally. However the days of the Mk.V with the 'HM' code were nearly over. A couple more operational flights were carried out like on 11 February when the Squadron provided an escort to Vultee Vengeances. On return F/O Raymond Crossfield (RCAF) swung on the runway while landing. He escaped injury but his Spitfire – MA902 – was too badly damaged to be repaired. A couple of days later the Squadron switched definitively to the Mk.VIII after having flown close to 500 sorties and claiming over 30 Japanese aircraft confirmed as destroyed or probably destroyed. This made 136 Squadron the most successful Spitfire Mk.V unit in the Far East.

Claims - 136 Squadron (Confirmed and Probable)

Date	Pilot	SN	Origin	Type	Serial	Code	Nb	Cat.
05.12.43	F/L Eric **Brown**	RAF No.102413	RAF	Ki 21	**LZ939**	HM-N	1.0	C
26.12.43	F/Sgt Robert W. **Cross**	RAF No.924906	RAF	Ki 43		HM-F	2.0	C
	F/L John D. **Rudling**	NZ41714	RNZAF	Ki 21	**MA386**		1.0	C
31.12.43	F/L Arthur C. **Conway**	RAF No.104547	RAF	Ki 21	**JL319**	HM-B	2.0	C
				Ki 43	**JL319**	HM-B	1.0	C
				Ki 43	**JL319**	HM-B	1.0	P
	F/Sgt Robert W. **Cross**	RAF No.924906	RAF	Ki 21		HM-F	1.0	C
				Ki 43			1.0	C
	F/Sgt Reginald J. **Clarke**	NZ412205	RNZAF	Ki 21			1.0	C
	F/O Greville J. **Moorhouse**	RAF No.111999	RAF	Ki 43			1.0	C
	P/O Denis E. W. **Garvan**	Aus.411700	RAAF	Ki 21			1.0	C
				Ki 21			1.0	P
	F/O Vernon B.G. **Butler**	Can./J.16525	RCAF	Ki 21			1.0	C
				Ki 21			1.0	P
	F/L Lorne H. **LeCraw**	Can./J.6183	RCAF	Ki 21			1.0	C
	F/L Eric **Brown**	RAF No.102413	RAF	Ki 21	**MA899**		1.0	C
				Ki 21	**MA899**		1.0	P
15.01.44	P/O Denis E. W. **Garvan**	Aus.411700	RAAF	Zero	**MH637**	HM-P	2.0	C
				Zero	**MH637**	HM-P	1.0	P
	F/L Arthur C. **Conway**	RAF No.104547	RAF	Zero	**JL319**	HM-B	1.0	C
	F/O Greville J. **Moorhouse**	RAF No.111999	RAF	Zero	**MH638**	HM-Q	1.0	C
	F/O Dudley J. **Barnett**	Aus.405461	RAAF	Zero	**MA902**	HM-T	1.0	C
	F/Sgt Frank E. **Wilding**	RAF No.1015523	RAF	Zero	**MA384**	HM-U	1.0	P
20.01.44	S/L Alexander N. **Constantine**	RAF No.40893	RAF	Ki 43	**MA383**	HM-C	1.0	C
				Ki 43	**MA383**	HM-C	3.0	P
	P/O Denis E. W. **Garvan**	Aus.411700	RAAF	Ki 43	**JL303**	HM-S	1.0	C
				Ki 43	**MA675**	HM-S	1.0	P
	F/Sgt William L. **Cousens**	Aus.421911	RAAF	Ki 43	**MA364**	HM-O	1.0	C
	F/Sgt Kenneth **Bunting**	RAF No.1111872	RAF	Ki 43	**MA902**	HM-T	1.0	C
	F/O Charles G. **Beale**	NZ403560	RNZAF	Ki 43	**MA384**	HM-U	1.0	C

Total: 35.0

Summary of the aircraft lost on Operations - 136 Squadron

Date	Pilot	S/N	Origin	Serial	Code	Fate
05.12.43	F/L Eric **Brown**	RAF No.102413	RAF	**LZ939**	HM-N	-
26.12.43	F/L John D. **Rudling**	NZ41714	RNZAF	**MA386**		-
31.12.43	F/L Eric **Brown**	RAF No.102413	RAF	**MA899**		-
15.01.44	F/O Derek E. **Fuge**	RAF No.111995	RAF	**MA851**	HM-K	†
20.01.44	F/Sgt Peter F. **Kennedy**	RAF No.544902	(IRE)/RAF	**MA365**	HM-E	†
05.02.44	F/Sgt Arthur B. **Kearon**	RAF No.540606	(IRE)/RAF	**JG714**	HM-R	†
11.02.44	F/O Raymond J. **Crossfield**	CAN./J.21577	RCAF	**MA902**	HM-T	-

Total: 7

Dudley Barnett in his Spitfire Mk.V exchanges pleasantries with F/Sgt Wilding. Barnett was an English-born Australian had served with 136 Sqn since March 1943. He left in June 1944 and ended the war with 292 Sqn.
(Drew Harrison)

Summary of the aircraft lost by accident - 136 Squadron

Date	Pilot	S/N	Origin	Serial	Code	Fate
15.11.43	F/Sgt Reginald J. **Clarke**	NZ412205	RNZAF	**MA288**	HM-G	-

Total: 1

Victories - confirmed or probable claims: 21.0

First operational sortie:
26.10.43
Last operational sortie:
14.03.44

Number of sorties: ca. **800**

Total aircraft written-off: 3

Aircraft lost on operations: 2
Aircraft lost in accidents: 1

Squadron code letters:
AF

COMMANDING OFFICERS

S/L Patrick J.T. STEPHENSON	RAF No.81343	(IRE)/RAF	...	...

SQUADRON USAGE

This squadron arrived in India in March 1942 as a Hurricane unit. In Autumn 1943 607 Squadron was led by S/L Patrick Stephenson who had been just awarded the DFC for his long service with the unit. It was a true Commonwealth squadron with 34 pilots including nine Canadians, six Australians and one Burmese by November that year. The Squadron was sent to Alipore to begin its conversion to the Spitfire. The first machines (MA368 and MA391) arrived on the 14th at dusk and the pilots hurried out in force to welcome them. The first flights were done on the 19 November when eight pilots soloed on the Spitfire. The CO, of course, was the first – he flew MA638 on this occasion. By the end of the month more Spitfires had arrived (JG865, JL321, JL334, LZ971, LZ972, LZ975, MA290, MA296, MA341, MA672, MA674, MA676, MA677, MA686, MA688) while the Hurricanes kept flying for a little while. Soon, though, the Squadron had its full complement of Spitfires.

607 Squadron left Alipore in October, with 13 Spitfires, for Armada Road where an intensive training course was arranged. Over

The Australian Wilfred Goold of NewSouth Wales, who joined 607 Sqn in England during November 1941 before the unit shipped out to the Far East. He became one of the squadron's most successful pilots flying Spitfire Mk.Vs and continued to make claims later piloting the Mk.VIII. He was repatriated in June 1944 and was later awarded the DFC.
(via Andrew Thomas)

450 hours were flown that month in training. October also saw the first operational flights. The first was an uneventful scramble early in the afternoon of the 26th flown by F/O Gilbert Coons (RCAF) and Sgt Peter Moore of A Flight. Over the next two days another scramble took place without result. In November 607 Squadron was relocated to Ramu and, during the month, 46 sorties were completed and 10 scrambles were recorded. All were uneventful and, generally speaking, little air activity was reported – only 270 hours were flown in training and on operations. Despite this low level of activity the Squadron suffered its first loss when F/O Alexander Fraser (RCAF) was killed while conducting an air test on LZ971.

Activity steadily increased in December and 350 hours were flown with two-thirds of that total on operations. The squadron responded to regular scrambles, which were still uneventful, and also strike missions, like as the 6 December attack on Akyab aerodrome, and convoy patrols which collectively explain the 227 sorties recorded that month. This total was helped when the British launched a ground offensive on 30 November and 607 Squadron was united with 136 Squadron in 165 Wing at Ramu under the leadership of W/C Jimmy Edson.

January 1944 began, like the previous months, with frustratingly uneventful scrambles. But things changed for the better on the 15th when the Squadron was called to cover 136 Squadron's Spitfires, providing 12 aircraft, and joining forces over Maungdaws. That day the Japanese returned in force to the Arakan Penisula with the 64th Sentai mounting several sweeps over the Maunggdaung-Buthidaung area. Furious dogfights took place and F/L William James claimed a 'Hamp' as probably destroyed, which was later confirmed, and also claimed two more aircraft as damaged. Also victorious that day were W/O Brian Bohane - RAAF - (with one confirmed kill and one damaged), F/Sgt Herman Saunby (one probable) and F/Sgt Peter Moore (one probable) while three Spitfires returned with damage. These were the aircraft flown by P/O Jack Yates, F/Sgt Peter Mann and F/Sgt Jonathon Haley (RAAF). The battle wasn't over. Ninety minutes later a second sweep, comprising eight Ki-43s, appeared. Five stayed above as cover while three went down to strafe British positions. The latter were caught by the Spitfires and all shot down while of the Ki-43s waiting above three were claimed as destroyed and one more probably destroyed with another damaged. The victorious pilots that day included F/O Derek Benson (with one confirmed), F/L Colin Doudy, S/L Patrick Lee, of 165 Wing, F/Sgt Clifford Curnock and F/Sgt Peter Moore while the Squadron CO claimed a probable kill. In all it was a very fruitful day for 607 Squadron. After a couple of quiet days the Squadron was again involved in aerial combat against the Japanese early on the 20th. 607 Squadron's Spitfires climbed, in conjunction with those of 136 Squadron, to 30,000 feet with the CO leading the formation. Enemy aircraft were seen over Mauggdaw flying at 10,000 feet with another formation at 18-24,000 – in all there were around 100 Japanese aircraft! In the ensuing engagement the CO was hit in the arm early in the fight and had to return to base leaving the leadership to S/L Lee. At the end of the combat 607 Squadron was able to claim five probable kills and three damaged but, later on, the claims made by F/L Michael Coombes and P/O Yates were confirmed. This time, sadly, the Japanese fighters were more successful than they had been previously and shot down and killed the New Zealander W/O George Sole. The rest of January remained quiet and the last sorties of the month took place on the 29th with an uneventful scramble flown by P/O Fernand Jolicoeur (RCAF) and P/O Francis Lloyd.

In February the fortunes of war changed. On the 5th two Spitfires took off to intercept a Dinah, a reconnaissance aircraft, which was shot down. F/O Coons and Sgt Benedict Neville (RCAF) shared the claim. An hour later nine 607 Squadron Spitfires followed eight 136 Squadron aircraft, which had scrambled 15 minutes earlier, and soon spotted fighters flying below them over Buthidaung. The pilots were able to add four aircraft claimed as damaged (two of them by S/L Lee). To prevent any new Japanese incursions the Squadron organised standing patrols during the following days. On the 9th the Spitfires engaged Ki-43s over the Buthidaung area and combats occurred at all altitudes. F/L William James and P/O Yates each claimed one aircraft probably

destroyed and one damaged between them but, in return, F/Sgt Mann, flying Spitfire MA367, was killed. The next day 607 Squadron intercepted the escort for some Japanese bombers and two more damaged aircraft were claimed by S/L Lee and F/O Robert Bates (RCAF). An escort for Vengeances was provided that afternoon. Escort was again provided on the 13th, for Wellingtons this time, and two days later 607 Squadron scrambled once more over Buthidaung where more than 60 Japanese fighters were reported. The squadron, led by F/L 'Jimmy' James, were vectored towards Maungdaw and, in the following minutes, claimed one aircraft as probably destroyed and one as damaged. Four days later, on the 19th, 607 Squadron was called upon to intercept a mixed formation of Japanese bombers and fighters south-east of Akyab Island. F/L Colin Douby distinguished himself in claiming a Ki-43 probably destroyed and two more damaged while six others were claimed by other pilots (F/O Robert Bates - RCAF and F/Sgt Kenneth Longley claimed two each and F/L James and F/L Wilfred Goold - RAAF made single claims). The next day 607 Squadron was called on once more to provide escort to Hurricanes of 134 Squadron, and the following day to Vengeances, but the end of the month ended without incident and, in total, 470 hours on Spitfires were flown. On the 22nd, at 16.50, Spitfires were dispatched to patrol over Oyster Island and await further instructions. At 17.15 P/O Yates and Sgt Longley arrived to relieve the initial pair and were patrolling at 21,000 feet when at 17.55 they were advised by control of aircraft in the Akyab area. Longley spotted a twin-engined aircraft taxiing on Dabaing strip and another aircraft parked off the runway. A smoke generator was set off on the ground to obscure the airfield as soon as the British fighters appeared. Yates at once dived on the aircraft parked off the runway but encountered AA fire. As he committed to his strafing run he spotted four more aircraft in the circuit. One seemed to be trying to take-off so he fired on it and saw strikes all over the aircraft. At this point he spotted at least a dozen fighters in the circuit. Upon sighting these he and Longley fled pursued by six of the fighters which were soon outpaced. On returning to base he was duly credited with the aircraft he fired at.

In March, the Squadron continued to fly but less intensively – only interception scrambles were carried out, except on the 7th, when a sweep over Akyab was carried out, and the 14th, when the squadron provided escort for a Beaufighter returning home on one engine. This was the last of the operational sorties recorded on Spitfire Mk.Vs as the Squadron started operations on the very welcome Spitfire Mk.VIII the next day. The Squadron claimed 21 confirmed or probable victories in just over 800 sorties on the Mk.V and lost only two Spitfires to the Japanese.

From South Australia Colin Doudy was another long -serving pilot in 607 Sqn when it received its first Spitfire Mk.Vs. He was awarded the DFC in April 1945, and served in the post-war RAAF.
(Andrew Thomas)

Claims - 607 Squadron (Confirmed and Probable)

Date	Pilot	SN	Origin	Type	Serial	Code	Nb	Cat.
15.01.44	F/L William D. JAMES	RAF No.113097	RAF	Ki 43	**MA857**	AF-G	1.0	P
	W/O Brian J. BOHANE	AUS.405614	RAAF	Ki 43	**MA672**		1.0	C
	F/Sgt Herman C. SAUNBY	RAF No.1203376	RAF	Ki 43	**MA677**	AF-T	1.0	P
	F/Sgt Peter E.D. MOORE	RAF No.1333351	RAF	Ki 43	**JL321**	AF-K	1.0	P
	F/O Derek A. BENSON	RAF No.124322	RAF	Ki 43	**MA368**		1.0	C
	F/L Colin T. DOUDY	AUS.403127	RAAF	Ki 43	**LZ975**	AF-J	1.0	C
	S/L Patrick H. LEE	RAF No.39796	RAF	Ki 43		AF-Q	1.0	C
	F/Sgt Clifford A.N. CURNOCK	RAF No.1380200	RAF	Ki 43	**MH299**	AF-A	1.0	C
	F/Sgt Peter E.D. MOORE	RAF No.1333351	RAF	Ki 43	**JL321**		1.0	C
	S/L Patrick J.T. STEPHENSON	RAF No.81343	(IRE)/RAF	Ki 43	**MA857**	AF-G	1.0	P
20.01.44	F/L Michael W. COOMBES	RAF No.33561	RAF	Ki 43	**JL321**	AF-K	1.0	C
	P/O Jack N. YATES	RAF No.159463	RAF	Ki 43	**MH299**	AF-A	1.0	C
	F/O Wilfried A. GOOLD	AUS.403135	RAAF	Ki 43	**MA677**	AF-T	1.0	P
	F/Sgt Herbert SAUNBY	RAF No.1094826	RAF	Ki 43	**MA686**		1.0	P
	F/Sgt Peter E.D. MOORE	RAF No.1333351	RAF	Ki 43	**LZ975**	AF-J	1.0	P
05.02.44	F/O Gilbert L. COONS	CAN./J.40094	RCAF	Ki 46	**MA347**	AF-Z	0.5	C
	Sgt Joseph B. NEVILLE	CAN./R.123337	RCAF		**MA696**	AF-O	0.5	C
09.02.44	F/L William D. JAMES	RAF No.113097	RAF	Ki 43	**MH302**	AF-D	1.0	P
	P/O Jack N. YATES	RAF No.159463	RAF	Ki 43	**MH299**	AF-A	1.0	P
15.02.44	F/L William D. JAMES	RAF No.113097	RAF	Ki 43	**MH302**	AF-D	1.0	P
21.02.44	F/L Colin T. DOUDY	AUS.403127	RAAF	Ki 43	**JL331**	AF-J	1.0	P
22.02.44	P/O Jack N. YATES	RAF No.159463	RAF	Zero	**MH639**	AF-F	1.0	C

Total: 21.0

Summary of the aircraft lost on Operations - 607 Squadron

Date	Pilot	S/N	Origin	Serial	Code	Fate
20.01.44	W/O George SOLE	NZ404418	RNZAF	**MA296**	AF-S	†
09.02.44	F/Sgt Peter R. MANN	RAF No.1380272	RAF	**MA367**		†

Total: 2

Summary of the aircraft lost by accident - 607 Squadron

Date	Pilot	S/N	Origin	Serial	Code	Fate
20.11.43	F/O Alexander M. FRASER	CAN./J.16528	RCAF	**LZ971**		†

Total: 1

Victories - confirmed or probable claims: 17.0

First operational sortie: 04.10.43	**Number of sorties:** ca. **1,630**
Last operational sortie: 12.07.44	**Total aircraft written-off: 20**

Aircraft lost on operations: 12
Aircraft lost in accidents: 8

Squadron code letters:
KW

COMMANDING OFFICERS

S/L Robert H. HOLLAND	RAF No.33487	RAF	...	01.02.44
S/L David W. McCORMACK	Aus.400232	RAAF	01.02.44	...

SQUADRON USAGE

The first unit to receive Spitfires in the Far East was actually 615 Squadron. The squadron had been sent to the region in June 1942 to reinforce the RAF against the Japanese advance and had fought with Hurricanes since then. Its CO was S/L Robert Holland who was a former Battle of Britain veteran with 92 Squadron with which he was awarded the DFC. He had been posted to 615 Squadron in 1942 for his second tour. The squadron was located at Alipore when its first Spitfires arrived in early October. Of the 32 pilots on strength all were British but for four Australians, three Canadians and two New Zealanders. Work to prepare for the new aircraft had already begun the previous month. The last flights on Hurricanes were recorded on 1 October and from the next day all pilots started to fly their new mount. While the squadron was still working up on the type, with only 13 hours logged so far, F/L Paul G. Louis, the A Flight CO, flying MA263, was called on to carry out the first Spitfire scramble in India. Louis took off at 11.20 and returned one hour later. However it was the pilots of 136 Squadron (still flying Hurricanes) who were able to intercept the Japanese reconnaissance aircraft and damage it. F/L Louis was a very experienced pilot who, the previous June, had added the DFC to the DFM he earned in England in December 1941. One week later, on the 11th, two pilots were dispatched on a scramble. F/L Brian T. Verry (RNZAF, B Flight commander), in JL320, and F/L Graham 'Porky' Falconer (RAAF), in MA263, took off at 14.10 to intercept an aircraft which proved to be friendly. The following day four more aircraft were scrambled in two pairs (one at 10.50 the other at 11.00) but the enemy aircraft turned back before the interception could be made. Over the next two days other aircraft were scrambled - one on the 13th and two on the 14th - but, on the 16th, the Spitfires were sent to Armada Road to do their air-firing training. By the end of the month close to 425 hours had been flown (including a couple of minutes in operations).

David McCormack, DFC & Bar, an Australian from Victoria, officially took command of 615 Sqn on 1 February 1944, at the peak of its Spitfire Mk.V usage. He was an old hand having completed a first tour with the squadron between May 1941 and March 1943. His second tour commenced in January 1944 and he was killed in a flying accident in August, piloting his new Spitfire Mk.VIII (LV742)-this only a month after the sqn began re-equipping with the updated machines.

On 1 November the Squadron returned to Chittagong fully operational and, two days later a scramble and an escort for Vengeances were carried out. On the 8th the Spitfire destroyed its first Japanese aircraft in the Far East when F/L Louis in JL108, accompanied by F/O Lawrence Weggery (RNZAF) in MA349, took off at 07.45 to intercept a Dinah reconnaissance aircraft. They were able to catch it at 25,000 feet over Chittagong at 08.12 and it was seen diving to the ground in flames nine minutes later. Two days later another Dinah was shot down by F/Sgt Arthur Hyde. He caught the aircraft at 29,000 feet, out to sea off Chittagong, and after a running fight lasting six minutes the burning enemy aircraft dived vertically into the sea. It was not the only major event of the day, however, as the squadron had to record the loss of two Spitfires. First was Sgt Grenier of Ceylon who failed to return from cannon firing into the sea and, luckily, the Australian F/O George Andrews escaped without major injuries when he crashed on returning from a night training flight. One week later the squadron shot down a third Dinah. F/O Kevin Gannon (RAAF) was the successful pilot. More interceptions were carried out over the following days without results until the 23rd when the Squadron was engaged in a major combat against a Japanese formation of over 18 aircraft. Following the recent losses of Dinahs the Japanese had decided to attempt the destruction of some of the newcomers responsible. Thus Ki-43s were sent in the hope of engaging combat and destroy some of them. On this day the tactic was successful. While the RAF took off in numbers to catch the Japanese, 615 Squadron contributing 10 Spitfires, the Ki-43s were able to shoot down P/O Hugh Leonard (RCAF) who fortunately survived. The Spitfires did not make any claims against the Japanese. The latter increased the pressure and launched a raid over the Arakan on the 29th, with 12 Ki-48s escorted by nine Ki-43s, so the RAF scrambled Hurricanes from five squadrons and twelve Spitfires from 615 Squadron. This time luck was with the Allies who claimed one Ki-48 probably destroyed (P/O Arthur Carroll) and four fighters damaged. November ended the following day with an uneventful scramble but this month had been busy for 615 Squadron with three confirmed victories and one more probable, in close to 200 sorties, for the loss of two Spitfires and one pilot to the Japanese.

Lawrence Weggery who named his Spitfires after his wife. His first, in which he made his first claim, MA349/KW-D 'Verna June', was lost when flown by another pilot. Here he is in his Spitfire MA292/KW-D, with which he made his second claim. *(SLE Weggery via Paul Sortehaug)*

The first three weeks of December were even more intense with over 100 sorties carried out – though these were largely uneventful. On 13 December the Squadron moved forward and was stationed at Dohazari, east of Chittagong. The Squadron had to wait until Boxing Day for further action when two Australian pilots, F/O 'Bill' Andrews and F/Sgt Henry 'Chat' Chatfield, scrambled at 11.15 to intercept what was first thought to be a reconnaissance aircraft. However their target suddenly increased to 40 or 50 enemy aircraft which were part of a big Japanese raid. The two pilots didn't hesitate to attack and in the ensuing combat Andrews claimed one Oscar and one Sally destroyed and one more damaged. These aircraft increased his tally to three aircraft destroyed after having shot down a Japanese bomber the previous April while flying Hurricanes. 'Chat' Chatfield claimed his first two victories by downing two Sally bombers. The rest of the Squadron took off 20 minutes after the two Australians as back up but most of the pilots didn't make contact. However F/O Albert Valentine and Sgt Donald Wright (RCAF) had become separated from the squadron in cloud at 29,000 feet. Those two eventually made contact with Japanese bombers, and were preparing to attack, when they were surprised by Japanese fighters who shot down and killed the Canadian. On the last day of the year the Squadron was again scrambled with twelve aircraft, and contact was made, but only P/O Hugh Leonard (RCAF) was able to make a claim on a Ki-43 which he damaged.

January 1944 was rather quiet and operational activity was only half that of December. Nevertheless the Squadron added one more Dinah to its tally on 16 January. The aircraft was shot down in flames 70 miles east of the airfield at Dohazari by F/L Louis and F/O Weggery. Louis took temporary command of the Squadron from 20 January when S/L Holland left for a Staff College course. Holland's permanent successor was the very experienced Australian S/L David McCormack who had been awarded the DFC and Bar with the Squadron during a previous tour. The first week of February continued in the same vein but on the 9th the Japanese decided to make an air strike with fighters over the RAF airstrips. The Squadron took off at 9.35 to join the mêlée at the end of which W/O Huon Chandler (RNZAF) claimed one Ki-43 destroyed while F/Sgt John Hill and Sgt Charles Watson claimed two aircraft damaged each. In addition F/L Verry, F/O Wilfred Bond (RCAF) and P/O John Oldham each claimed one aircraft damaged against no loss even though the aircraft flown by P/O John Gibbins (JL334) returned with some damage. The following day the Squadron was called on to fulfil various missions, scrambles and escorts and on the 25th the Squadron received orders to move to Nazir, south of Cox's Bazaar. During the take-off to the new station the auxiliary petrol tank of MA263, flown by P/O Arthur Carroll, fell off. The Spitfire stalled and the undercarriage collapsed as the aircraft crashed at the end of the runway.

Life at Nazir didn't change that much in terms of operations except that the Squadron was able to launch some offensive sweeps on Japanese positions. By that time 615 Squadron was the sole Spitfire unit still flying the Mk.V and during the month it began to inherit some former 607 Squadron aircraft. The Squadron was now based at Silchar West. In April 615 experienced an intense period of operational activity with over 400 sorties, mainly escorts and offensive sweeps, carried out. On the 12th Sgt Hill burst a tyre on take-off for a routine patrol and his Spitfire tipped onto its nose. The aircraft was later declared to be damaged beyond economical repair while Hill sustained head injuries.

There was nothing of interest to report until the 19th when the Squadron was sent to Wangging on readiness. The aircraft piloted by Sgt Charles Watson swung on take-off and hit a ditch after a tyre burst. The aircraft was a total write-off but the pilot fortunately

Poor quality tires led to many accidents including MH6038 flown by Sgt Hill. Fortunately the pilot escaped injuries but his Spitfire was good for little more than scrapping. *(HB Chatfield via Drew Harrison)*

escaped injuries. Six days later three Spitfires, which were still at Silchar awaiting inspection, were ordered to scramble at 08.00 to intercept nine Oscars flying at 5,000 feet 40 miles south of the airfield. The combat was short and furious but F/L Gannon claimed a probable and F/L 'Porky' Falconer claimed one damaged. The next day more successes were added after the Squadron was scrambled at 09.30. The Squadron had returned from a sweep only 40 minutes earlier and the aircraft had been refuelled and re-armed just in time to make the interception. This time 615 Squadron fought against 20 Oscars of which one each was probably destroyed by the CO and Flying Officer Andrews (RAAF) while F/L Weggery claimed two damaged and P/O Carroll made a single damaged claim.

Early in May 615 Squadron made a big move north to be stationed at Dergaon, about 20 miles west of Jorhat, and operational activity resumed on the 12th. Four days later the Squadron recorded the loss of P/O Thomas Stothard who was killed while taking off from Johrat. Another loss occurred on the 20th when the aircraft of P/O Chandler (RNZAF) turned over on returning from an uneventful scramble at the end of the morning. Shortly after mid-day seven Spitfires provided escort for Dakotas without incident. On the 23rd the Squadron moved south and was sent to Palel, not far from Imphal. Two days later nine Spitfires scrambled to intercept Japanese fighters (Ki-43s) which were only a few miles from the base. Many claims were made - one fighter probably destroyed by F/Sgt Charles Watson while S/L McCormack claimed two damaged. Watson's success was costly for him, however, as he had to make a forced-landing seven miles north of Imphal because of a glycol leak. He was injured in the process. On the 29th the Squadron, led by the CO, took off again to intercept over 30 approaching enemy fighters and in the ensuing combat four fighters were claimed as damaged including one by the CO, one by Gannon and two by Chandler. In return the Japanese were able to shot down and kill a newcomer, Australian Sgt Henry Young, while McCormack had to crash land at Sapam due to an internal glycol leak. Furthermore he had to be admitted to hospital with injuries but returned to the Squadron on 5th June. His aircraft, MH640, was investigated and was later declared irreparable and struck off charge in July. On 30 May 615 Squadron lost another Spitfire, MH301, by accident. The aircraft had taken off with new tyres made by the Goodrich Tyre Co of Durban (South Africa) and W/O Roy Layfield (RAAF), posted in ten days previously, had been chosen to try the new tyres. The starboard tyre burst on take-off and on landing the aircraft swung into soft ground, hit a ditch and turned over marking an end to the career of MH301 as well as the tyres which were eventually condemned.

After a quiet May, with less than 150 sorties flown, June saw 615's workload steadily increase with over 300 sorties carried out, with more *Rhubarb* or escort missions completed, and many targets on the ground destroyed. But that had a high cost as it was the worst month the Squadron had suffered since the introduction of the Spitfire the previous autumn. The problems started on the 8th when F/Sgt Eric Kennedy (RAAF) taxied into a ditch after returning from an escort of a Dakota. The pilot escaped unhurt but his Spitfire was suitable only for scrap. One week later 615 Squadron escorted Dakotas and on the return journey very poor weather conditions were encountered. Three pilots, P/O Arthur Hyde, F/Sgt Kennedy and F/Sgt James McKay, were posted missing in what was a severe blow for the squadron. Two days later the Squadron was called on to perform an offensive recce very early in the morning and later that morning carried out a standing patrol (also called a *Z patrol*) during which they were diverted to intercept over 20 'bandits' flying at 8,000 feet. Combat followed and 615 Squadron (F/L Gannon and F/Sgt Chatfield) claimed two Oscars destroyed and one probably destroyed (F/O Cyril Buch). But those successes cost W/O John Payne (RAAF), presumed shot down and killed by Ki-43s. He fortunately survived and later returned to 615 with an incredible tale of survival. Two days later his twin brother, F/Sgt Alfred Payne, was posted to the Squadron

Among the many Australians serving with 615 Sqn when the Spitfire arrived was Kevin Gannon, from Queensland, who had arrived in October 1942. He took command of a flight in May 1944 and, when his tour ended in November 1944, he was posted as a flying instructor to 151 OTU at Peshawar in India.

Two successfurl Australian pilots; in cockpit, Geoffrey Andrew from New South Wales and standing, Harold Chatfield from Victoria. Both survived the war, Andrew serving with 79 Sqn, RAAF, in the Pacific.
(Andrew Thomas)

Left, Mervyn 'Mud' Fullford of New South Wales, Australia, completed a first tour in Europe with 66 Sqn. He started a second tour with 615 Sqn in June 1944, at the very end of the usage of the Spitfire Mk.V. He was tour-expired in March 1945 and became a test pilot at No.308 MU.
(HB Chatfield via Drew Harrison)

and therefore wouldn't miss the chance to fly on operations with his brother. Three days later, while carrying out a *Rhubarb* mission led by F/L Gannon, his wingman , F/O Thomas Kelley (RCAF), failed to return. During the mission he reported engine trouble and was seen crashing into trees at the edge of a field after which the aircraft was seen to catch fire.

While nothing worthy of note took place on the operational side on the 19th, the pilots of 615 Squadron were happy to see the first two Mk.VIIIs arrive at the Squadron that day, promising a new era for the squadron as the Mk.Vs were at the end of their operational career everywhere including in India. On the 23rd, two more Mk.VIIIs followed increasing to six by the end of the month. The Squadron flew on both types during the first fortnight of July, progressively giving up the Mk.Vs. On the 12th, two pairs took off at 07.00 for a *Rhubarb* mission, the first pair led by F/O Hugh Leonard (RCAF), the second by F/O Arthur Carroll, but the four Spitfires (MH302, MA696, MA852, MA857) had to return early due to bad weather. When they landed, it marked an end to the operational history of the Spitfire Mk.V in Far East. As for 615 Squadron alone, paradoxically, while the unit was the first to be equipped with the Mk.V, it claimed the fewest victories while sustaining the greatest losses.

11 Australians, almost half of 615 Sqn, in the summer of 1944. L-R: P/O Macolm T.W. Pain (†10.08.44); W/O John Payne, W/O Roy S.M. Layfield, F/O Mervyn Fullford, F/L Graham Falconer, the OC S/L David W. McCormack (†10.08.44), F/L Kevin F. Gannon, W/O Alan L. Chappell (†10.08.44), W/O Albert L. Whiteman, F/Sgt Harold B. Chatfield and W/O Alfred A; Payne, John Payne's twin brother.

Lawrence Weggery in his Spitire with which he made his second claim. Note the large silver fern under the pipes, leaving no one in doubt as to his nationality.

Claims - 615 Squadron (Confirmed and Probable)

Date	Pilot	SN	Origin	Type	Serial	Code	Nb	Cat.
08.11.43	F/L Paul G. LOUIS	RAF No.113346	RAF	Ki 46	JL108	KW-F	0.5	C
	F/O Sydney L.E. WEGGERY	NZ41968	RNZAF		MA349	KW-D	0.5	C
10.11.43	F/Sgt Arthur R. HYDE	RAF No.924833	RAF	Ki 46	JL334	KW-Y	1.0	C
16.11.43	F/O Kevin F. GANNON	Aus.404563	RAAF	Ki 46	MA388	KW-O	1.0	C
29.11.43	P/O Arthur G. CARROLL	RAF No.158780	RAF	Ki 48	MA263	KW-M	1.0	P
26.12.43	F/O Geoffrey W. ANDREWS	Aus.402932	RAAF	Ki 43	MA290	KW-R	1.0	C
				Ki-48	MA290	KW-R	1.0	C
	F/Sgt Harold B. CHATFIELD	Aus.401493	RAAF	Ki 48	JL320	KW-X	2.0	C
16.01.44	F/L Paul G. LOUIS	RAF No.113346	RAF	Ki 46	MH300	KW-A	0.5	C
	F/O Sydney L.E. WEGGERY	NZ41968	RNZAF		MA292		0.5	C
09.02.44	F/L Huon A. CHANDLER	NZ403944	RNZAF	Zero	MA670	KW-S	1.0	C
25.04.44	F/O Kevin F. GANNON	Aus.404563	RAAF	Ki 43	MA390	KW-B	1.0	P
26.04.44	S/L David W. McCORMACK	Aus.400232	RAAF	Ki 43	MH640	KW-G	1.0	P
	F/O Geoffrey W. ANDREWS	Aus.402932	RAAF	Ki 43	JL319		1.0	P
25.05.44	F/Sgt Charles M.G. WATSON	RAF No.771981	RAF	Ki 43	MH299		1.0	P
17.06.44	F/O Kevin F. GANNON	Aus.404563	RAAF	Ki 43	MA654	KW-R	1.0	C
	F/Sgt Harold B. CHATFIELD	Aus.401493	RAAF	Ki 43	MH303	KW-W	1.0	C
	F/O Cyril F. BUSH	RAF No.132175	RAF	Ki 43	MA857	KW-L	1.0	P

Total: 17.0

Summary of the aircraft lost on Operations - 615 Squadron

Date	Pilot	S/N	Origin	Serial	Code	Fate
23.11.43	P/O Hugh L.A. Leonard	Can./J.18103	RCAF	LZ972		-
26.12.43	W/O2 Donald L. Wright	Can./R.133306	RCAF	MA349	KW-D	†
12.04.44	F/Sgt John H. Hill	RAF No.1315173	RAF	MH638		-
20.05.44	P/O Huon A. Chandler	NZ405944	RNZAF	JL108	KW-F	-
25.05.44	Sgt Henry F. Watson	RAF No.1567648	RAF	MA292		Inj.
29.05.44	F/Sgt Henry K. Young	Aus.414148	RAAF	MA383		†
08.06.44	F/Sgt Eric D. Kennedy	Aus.420012	RAAF	MA390	KW-B	-
15.06.44	P/O Arthur R. Hyde	RAF No.169440	RAF	JL322	KW-V	†
	F/Sgt Eric D. Kennedy	Aus.420012	RAAF	JG865		†
	F/Sgt James B. McKay	RAF No.1387314	RAF	MA694		†
17.06.44	W/O John I. Payne	Aus.409953	RAAF	MA284		-
20.06.44	F/O Thomas Kelley	Can./J.16429	RCAF	MH302		†

Total: 12

New-Zealander Huon 'Chan' Chandler, one of the few Kiwis who served in 615 Sqn during the Spitfire Mk.V era. He had previously claimed a Japanese bomber destroyed and one more damaged on Hurricanes and was awarded the DFC. After completing his tour, in June 1944, he attended a Thunderbolt conversion course, but did not proceed to an operational squadron.
(HA Chandler via Paul Sortehaug)

Summary of the aircraft lost by accident - 615 Squadron

Date	Pilot	S/N	Origin	Serial	Code	Fate
10.11.43	Sgt Guy B.C. Grenier [1]	RAF No.771978	RAF	LZ973		†
	F/O George W. Andrews	Aus.402932	RAAF	MA650	KW-S	-
25.02.44	P/O Arthur G. Carroll	RAF No.158780	RAF	MA263	KW-M	-
19.04.44	F/Sgt Charles M.G. Watson	RAF No.771981	RAF	MA670	KW-S	-
16.05.44	F/O Thomas K. Stothard	RAF No.150018	RAF	JL320	KW-X	†
30.05.44	W/O Roy S.M. Layfield	Aus.414244	RAAF	MH301	KW-Y	-

Total: 6

[1] born in Ceylon from SA parentage

Photos of the Spitfire Mk.V in the Far East are so rare that even poor quality examples warrant publication. Here Kevin Gannon is seated in MA654 KW-R, during the summer of 1944. The movement of this aircraft is not known prior to June 1944, when it was alloted to 615 Sqn to become Gannon's regular mount. It does not feature in records of the other two Spitfire Mk.V squadrons, 136 and 607. It was used only for a short time by 615 Sqn, which transitioned to the Spitfire Mk.VIII in the following weeks. *(H B Chatfield via Drew Harrison)*

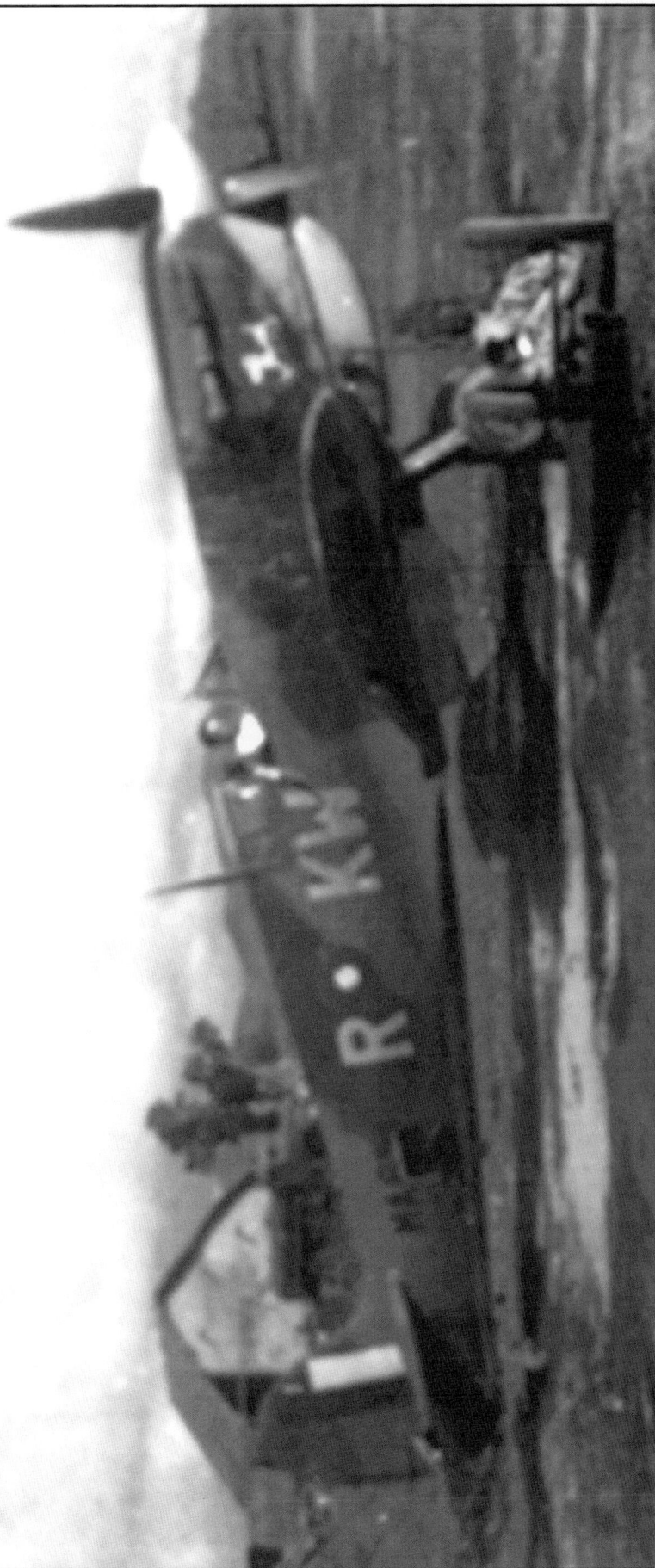

OTHER UNITS AND FINAL USE

Besides the operational use of the Mk.V in the Far East little is known about the Mark in this region. No records exist today so we can only attempt to ascertain with which other units the Mk.V served from scratch.

By Autumn 1944 at least eight were serving with the AFTU (Air Fighting Training Unit) at Armada Road. Indeed it is known that, early in November 1944, the pilots of No. 8 Sqn, IAF received orders to borrow eight Mk.Vs from the AFTU, when the Indian squadron arrived at Armada Road, and release their few Mk.VIII aircraft in exchange. At that time this squadron had one flight of IAF pilots, the other being largely composed of RAF pilots, and the CO was New Zealander S/L Ian A. Sutherland. The squadron was under conversion to the Spitfire Mk.VIII at the time but it was decided it would be preferable to train the pilots on the Mk.V first before continuing on the Mk.VIII. The first three were received on the 9th allowing six pilots of 8 Squadron IAF to make their first solo on the Mk.V that day. The following day one more Mk.V was exchanged for Mk.VIIIs and more pilots were able to fly the Mk.V. It is not certain, however, if 8 Squadron IAF received the final Mk.V due as, on the 13th, after discussions, it was established that the Indian pilots had flown enough on the Mk.V and the process stopped. This decision arrived too late for MA672 which was wrecked in a flying accident the following day after an engine failure after take-off. White fumes were seen pouring from the exhaust As the pilot, F/O Syed Hussain (IAF), tried to climb to 800 feet and make a turn to return to base. The engine seized before he could and he was obliged to make a forced landing five miles north west of Armada Road. He escaped injury but the Spitfire was later declared un-repairable and was converted to components. The Squadron received its former Mk.VIIIs back on the 18th and it is presumed that the surviving Mk.Vs were returned to the AFTU.

It is also known that the AFTU was not the only training unit to have used the Mk.V – 151 OTU seems to have used a couple of them when a Spitfire Flight was formed, as well as 3 RFU (Refresher Flying Unit) - the latter well into 1945 as two accidents can attest. The first of these took place on 1 June when Sgt Hallett (flying MA677) had to make a forced landing after an engine failure just after take-off, with no consequences for the pilot, and the second (MA393) was on 9 August under similar circumstances but this time the pilot, Sgt Hewlett, was injured.

As with all other aircraft some Spitfire Mk.Vs were lost while being ferried like JL331, which crashed during the flight taking it to a Maintenance Unit after its use with 607 Squadron, or MH639 on 5 January 1945. However there is one really unexplained loss - that of MA364. It is believed that a couple of Mk.Vs were also used, probably in the squadrons which were scheduled to convert to Spitfires, for familiarisation purposes. The only trace of that can be found in the accident card of MA364. The pilot, F/O Moolgavkhar of No.4 Squadron, IAF (retired as an Air Chief Marshall of the Indian Air Force in 1978), was doing a test flight (or probably his first solo as it was his first hour on the Spitfire) on this specific Mk.V. The engine cut out at 30 feet and the pilot landed wheels down, ran into shallow water and the Spitfire turned over injuring the pilot in the process. No.4 Squadron IAF was at that time flying Hurricanes and would convert to the Spitfire the following summer.

Date	Pilot	S/N	Origin	Serial	Code	Unit	Fate
07.06.44	W/O Ronald G. **BRYANT**	RAF No.1270477	RAF	**JL331**		22.FC	-
14.11.44	F/O Syed A. **HUSSAIN**	IND./1706	IAF	**MA672**		8 Sqn (IAF)	-
05.01.45	Lt Michael H. **DELPORT**	SAAF No.205593	SAAF	**MH639**		9.FU	-
15.01.45	F/O Hrushikesh **MOOLGAVKAR**	IND./1644	IAF	**MA364**		4 Sqn (IAF)	-

Probably taken in autumn 1944, Spitfire V MA286/G while belonged to the AFTU, which was using a handful of Spitfire Mk.Vs at that time. The AFTU adopted a single individual letter as identification, while the three operational squadrons, which were equipped with the Spitfire Mk.V, used their normal squadron two letter codes from the time they first arrived in the Far East. (HA Chandler via Paul Sortehaug)

Two other photos of AFTU's Spitfire Vs, MA286/G leading aircraft A and B. Spitfire 'B' is probably JL321. *(Tim Elkington)*

✝

IN MEMORIAM

Spitfire Mk.V
(Far East)

Name	Service No	Rank	Age	Origin	Date	Serial
FRASER, Alexander Malcolm	Can./J.16528	F/O	22	RCAF	20.11.43	LZ971
FUGE, Derek Edwin	RAF No.111995	F/O	21	RAF	15.01.44	MA851
GRENIER, Guy Bertram Christopher [1]	RAF No.771978	Sgt	22	RAF	10.11.43	LZ973
HYDE, Arthur Reginald	RAF No.169440	F/O	n/k	RAF	15.06.44	JL322
KEARON, Arthur Brodie	RAF No.54854	P/O	24	(IRE)/RAF	05.02.44	JG714
KELLEY, Thomas	Can./J.16429	F/O	22	RCAF	20.06.44	MH302
KENNEDY, Eric David	Aus.420012	W/O	24	RAAF	15.06.44	JG865
KENNEDY, Peter Francis	RAF No.54341	P/O	25	(IRE)/RAF	20.01.44	MA365
MANN, Peter Richard	RAF No.1380272	F/Sgt	21	RAF	09.02.44	MA367
McKAY, James Bordro	RAF No.1387314	F/Sgt	21	RAF	15.06.44	MA694
SOLE, George	NZ404418	W/O	23	RNZAF	20.01.44	MA296
STOTHARD, Thomas Kenneth	RAF No.150018	F/O	26	RAF	16.05.44	JL320
WRIGHT, Donald Lorimer	Can./R.133306	W/O2	20	RCAF	26.12.43	MA349
YOUNG, Henry Kenneth	Aus.414148	F/Sgt	21	RAAF	29.05.44	MA383

Total: 14

Australia: 2, Canada: 3, Ireland: 2, New Zealand: 1, United Kingdom: 6

[1] born in Ceylon from SA parentage

n/k: not known

Supermarine Spitfire Mk.V/Trop. LZ321
No. 607 (County of Durham) Squadron
Flight Lieutenant John K. 'Ken' CLARK (RCAF)
Ramu (Burma), January 1944

Supermarine Spitfire Mk.V/Trop. LZ975

No. 607 (County of Durham) Squadron
Flying Officer Colin T. DOUDY (RAAF)
Ramu (Burma), January 1944

GAETAN MARIE

Supermarine Spitfire Mk.V/Trop. MA292
No. 615 (County of Surrey) Squadron
Flying Officer Sydney L.E. 'Lawrence' WEGGERY (RNZAF)
Dohazari (India), January 1944

GAETAN MARIE

JL320

X

KW

Supermarine Spitfire Mk.V/Trop. JL320
No. 615 (County of Surrey) Squadron
Warrant Officer Huon A. 'Chan' CHANDLER (RNZAF)
Dohazari (India), December 1943

Supermarine Spitfire Mk.V/Trop. MA654
No. 615 (County of Surrey) Squadron
Flight Lieutenant Kevin F. GANNON (RAAF)
Palel (India), July 1944

GAETAN MARIE

Supermarine Spitfire Mk.V/Trop. MA368
No. 151 Operational Training Unit
Peshawar (India), January 1946

SQUADRONS! - The series

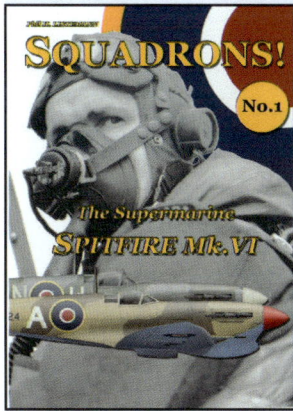

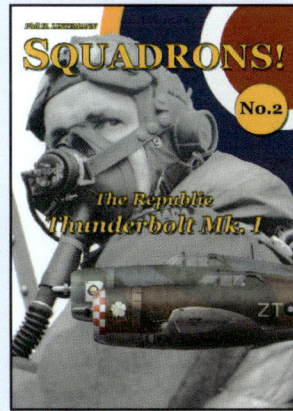

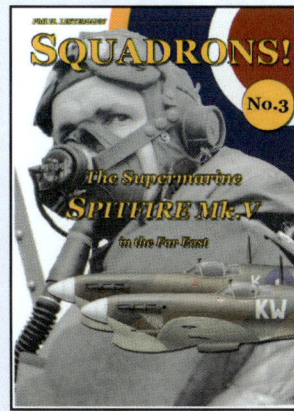

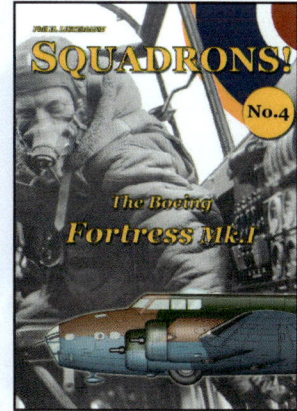

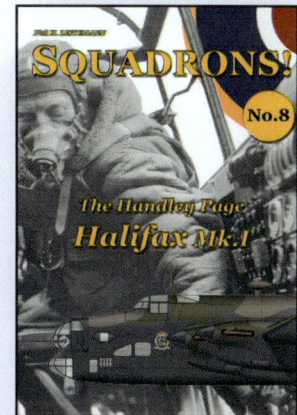

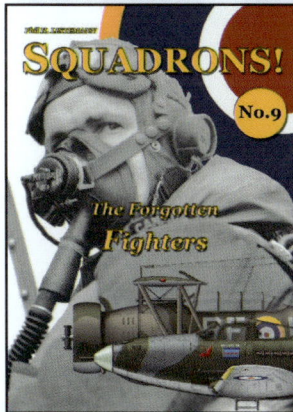

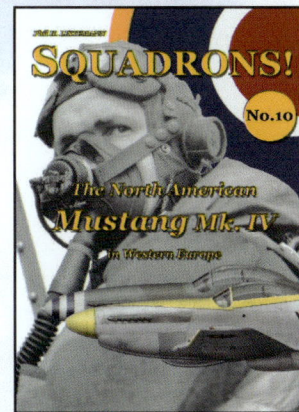

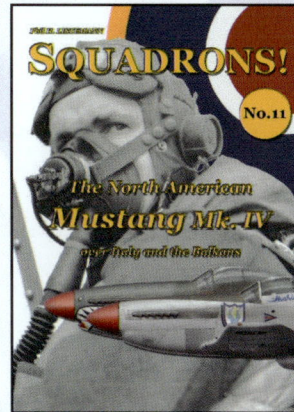

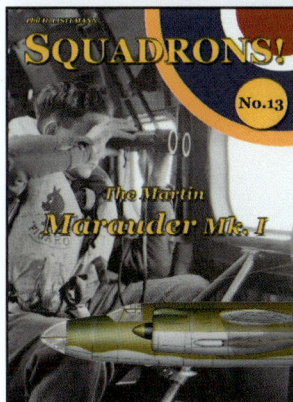

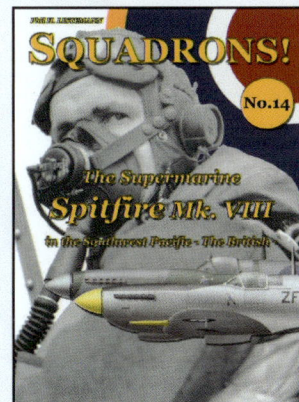

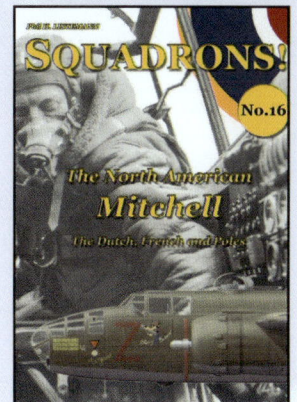

No.1 — The Supermarine *SPITFIRE Mk. VI*

No.2 — The Republic *Thunderbolt Mk. I*

No.3 — The Supermarine *SPITFIRE Mk. V* in the Far East

No.4 — The Boeing *Fortress Mk.I*

No.5 — The Supermarine *SPITFIRE Mk. XII*

No.6 — The Supermarine *SPITFIRE Mk. VII*

No.7 — The Supermarine *SPITFIRE F. 21*

No.8 — The Handley Page *Halifax Mk.I*

No.9 — The Forgotten *Fighters*

No.10 — The North American *Mustang Mk. IV* in Western Europe

No.11 — The North American *Mustang Mk. IV* over Italy and the Balkans

No.12 — The Supermarine *Spitfire Mk. XVI* - The British -

No.13 — The Martin *Marauder Mk. I*

No.14 — The Supermarine *Spitfire Mk. VIII* in the Southwest Pacific - The British -

No.15 — The Gloster *Meteor F. I & F. III*

No.16 — The North American *Mitchell* The Dutch, French and Poles

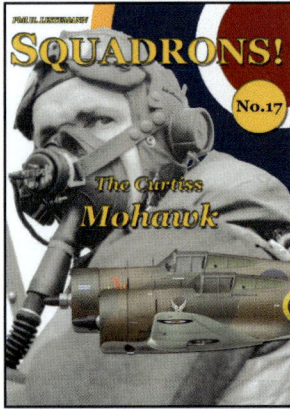

SQUADRONS! No.17

The Curtiss
Mohawk

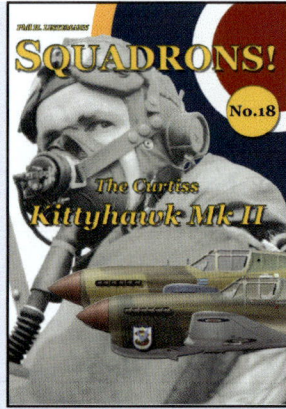

SQUADRONS! No.18

The Curtiss
Kittyhawk Mk II

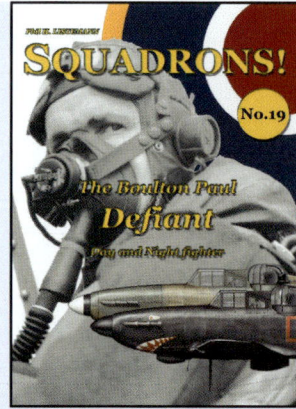

SQUADRONS! No.19

The Boulton Paul
Defiant

Day and Night fighter

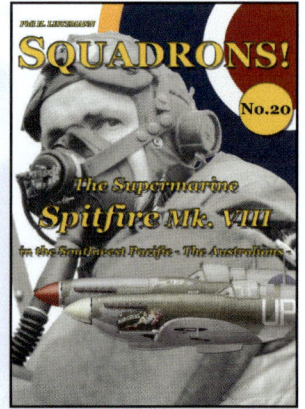

SQUADRONS! No.20

The Supermarine
Spitfire Mk. VIII

in the Southwest Pacific - The Australians

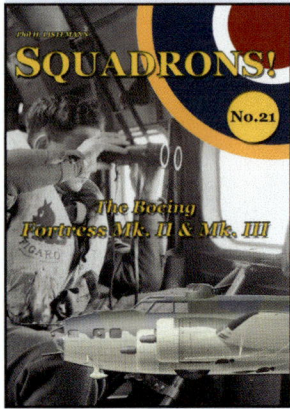

SQUADRONS! No.21

The Boeing
Fortress Mk. II & Mk. III

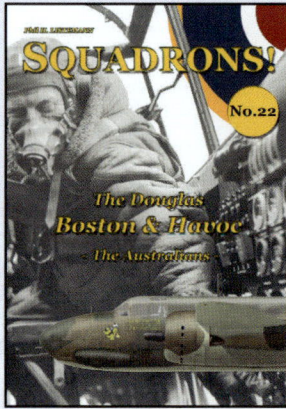

SQUADRONS! No.22

The Douglas
Boston & Havoc

- The Australians

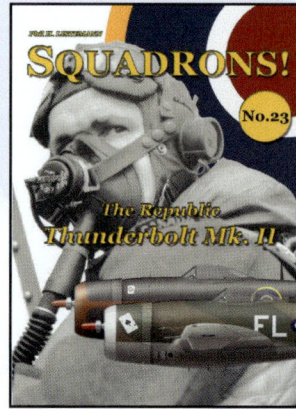

SQUADRONS! No.23

The Republic
Thunderbolt Mk. II

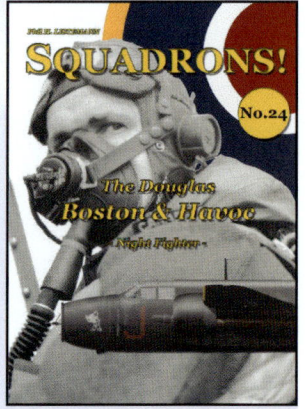

SQUADRONS! No.24

The Douglas
Boston & Havoc

- Night Fighter -

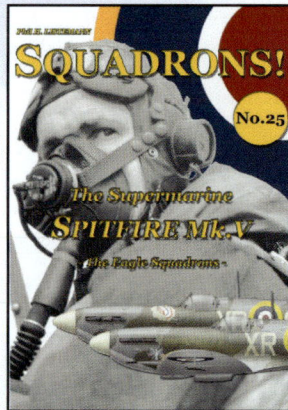

SQUADRONS! No.25

The Supermarine
SPITFIRE Mk. V

- The Eagle Squadrons -

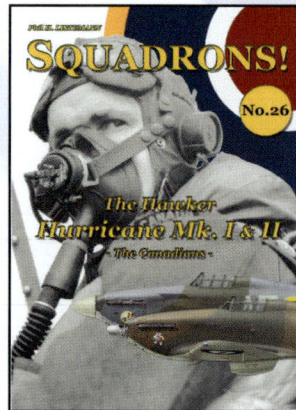

SQUADRONS! No.26

The Hawker
Hurricane Mk. I & II

- The Canadians -

Printed in Great Britain
by Amazon